The Santa Toy Story

My Christmas Wish

by; Cole Son

"Letters To Santa; Read by the

Campfire with his elves."

#ColeSon

#ColeSonBooks

Youtube: #ColeSonMusic

www.amazon.com/author/coleson

www.TheSantaToyStory.com

Prologue

It was almost time for Santa to embark on his tireless journey around the world to make sure every child's wish was fulfilled and that every kid had joy in their hearts. There was nothing that would hurt Santa more than knowing one single child had been missed and for this very reason, he was the only person in the world who could do this enormous job but not without the help of his magical team of elves and fairies. Yes, the fairies of the far north had joined with Santa and in this special story you will soon find out why

All year long Santa had been planning for this special day and it was now almost time as he walked towards the fireplace where he would sit every night with his favorite group of elves who were in command of making sure the right toys were being made and that the absolute correct wishes would be fulfilled on Christmas day. Gifts and presents did not come only in material form but also in the form of a wish and nothing could be missed to make sure every Christmas a perfect Christmas.

The job was getting even more difficult as the world grew bigger every year and more and more children were being born but Santa had full confidence in himself and his team. His precious reindeer and his elite team of magical elves would command an army of workers throughout the year, and the toy factory ran twenty-four hours a day to make sure they would not fail this Christmas.

As usual, Santa did his rounds around the elf village in the very far North Pole, making sure that everything was in perfect order. That the sleigh was in good working condition, that the reindeer were well-rested, and also that every single toy was accounted for according to the long list that was managed by Alabaster Snowball. He was smart and strict and had his eyes on every child's name on the planet.

But this Christmas there were a few surprises installed for Santa that would test his ability and bring him to the brink of failure. Could he overcome the obstacles he never expected would happen?

The snow was falling hard, and the wind was howling around the high cliffs of the ice cliffs that surrounded the elf village where they were working around the clock. This was the most important time of the year and the elves were almost out of time before Santa had to leave.

CHAPTERS

** 1 **

<u>THE FIRST LETTER</u>

The first letter Santa opened by the campfire was on January the first. That's when letters started arriving at the elf village from all over the world. Bags and bags full of letters, some thanking Santa for the gifts he had brought children and other letters with wishes for the next Christmas that seemed oh so long away. Santa had a big smile on his face as he remembered seeing the faces of so many kids who were filled with joy and happiness over the last Christmas season.

Oh, what a journey it was for Santa and his precious reindeer, through wind and hailstorms, over mountains and hot deserts and deep into the winter storms around the world. At times even Santa thought this was a job too tough for anyone, but he was so used to it that he made it every time. He knew however he might be coming to the end of his journeys.

Santa always felt relieved and happy after every single Christmas that he accomplished his task and made so many children happy. And if a child was happy their parents were happy too. Nothing hurt a parent more than if their child did not receive a present for Christmas. That was a feeling no parent wanted and certainly no child and that is why Santa's job was so very important.

It was the most important thing to do for planet earth every year, to make sure no kid went unhappy and even if there were request that were almost impossible, Santa would always find a solution somehow. After all, he was the solution to the problem. With the help of his reindeer, who had been with him for so long and the elves who were loyal to the task, Santa always had emergency measures in place incase something went wrong and many times things did go wrong.

If children could only imagine how difficult it was to make sure that all the kids who were good throughout the year received a gift or their wishes fulfilled, and that all the children who were bad, were not let down and still had a joyful Christmas, because in the end, Santa did not wanted to disappoint one single child on this earth.

The first letter Santa read were heart warming.

"Thank you, Santa, for having daddy return to us last Christmas. That was my greatest wish and you helped make it come true."

Tears welled up in his eyes of Santa as a satisfying smile broke across his wrinkled face and he stroke his white beard looking at the happy elves. A few clapped together their tiny hands in pure joy.

Around the campfire Santa was bundled together with more than fifteen elves in the cold night air as flakes of snow came down on them. They felt happy and emotional and proud, that they were part of something so important to this world. After all, healing the planet and all the people on earth was the most important thing to do. Not all the money in the world could buy happiness and joy. Sometimes a simple wish was all that was needed.

'Phew,' Santa thought as he wiped a feeling of relief from his thick white brow. 'That worked out.'

That was one of those wishes that were sometimes near impossible but miraculously that wish got fulfilled.

"Read us another wish, Santa," cried one of the elves.

He was the smallest of the fifteen elves that surrounded Santa at the campfire. Everywhere, ice

painted landscape as white as can be. It was a

fairytale setting with the tiny houses of the elves

snuggled into the tundra between the high pine trees

and hidden against the majestic mountains of ice that

surrounded them.

This was the far end of the North Pole and so

hidden that no human had ever been here. It was a

secret to everyone where Santa lived because if for

any reason someone had been disappointed they

could track Santa down and that would not be a good

thing but Santa knew no one was ever disappointed

under his watch.

"Yes, Santa, make us happy," said Pepper Minstix.

He was head of elf security and it was his job

to ensure that Santa's workshop stayed hidden and

protected in this magic world where dreams came

true. Pepper Minstix was entrusted with the

important job of watching out for the wellbeing and safety of Santa and the new Mrs. Claus. Yes, the old Mrs. Claus had passed away from old age and a new love had come into the life of Santa. The ice-princess of the very far North Pole, Evita, and they now had a son together who was soon to turn eighteen. His name was Kris Kringle and he was so handsome and athletic, Santa was surely proud of his only son. His son was very, very important because there was a great secret to be revealed that no one in the whole wide world had any idea about.

Pepper Minstix was dressed in military fatigues because he took his job very seriously and would go to any length to protect everyone in this village and keep it a secret forever. After all, the elf village and Santa's home was a very difficult place to find and if anyone tried, they would face the utmost treacherous path, of steep canyons, hidden ice gorges, tornado strength ice winds, making it a mere impossible task.

The only way to get in and out Santa's village safely was via the sleigh, and while during the year Santa was not using his sleigh, Pepper Minstix was entrusted to take it for important rides like taking the ice princess to visit her people in the highest peaks of the ice mountains where there existed an oasis of fairies and extremely beautiful creatures in a fairytale world.

After all, the reindeer needed their exercise as well or they would get fat and lazy and would not be able to accomplish the massive journey over the Christmas Holidays. Staying fit and healthy was very important for the reindeer.

The village of the ice princess was always a pleasure to visit as well for Santa and his son Kris. They had wonderful times in this fairytale land enjoying the company of the fairies and sometimes playing with the mythical creatures no human had seen in real life. From friendly dragons and mystical unicorns, to the tree people who could turn from trees into living beings and walk or run and even speak.

Here by the campfire were all the other important leaders of the village as well. Some joined by their wives, husbands and little elf children. They were so adorable with their pointy ears.

There was Alabaster Snowball who was in charge of the long, long list of children around the world and he knew who were good or bad. Albaster would decide by the end of the year which children deserved their presents and would get extra candy and treats. He was strict at times and even though Santa knew Albaster didn't make mistakes, Santa had a soft heart when it came to children and it would be hard for him not to award any child a gift.

Also at the campfire were, Bushy Evergreen, the skilled engineer and inventor the toy-making machine, Shinny Upatree, the oldest elf of the North Pole Village, even older than Santa and skinny and as wrinkled as an old apple. There was Sugarplum Mary with her four children, a tiny elf lady with dark hair and Asian eyes. She loved cooking and was in charge of creating all the world's treats and sweets for Christmas.

But don't mess with Mrs. Sugarplum. She was a master in kung Fu and could take on any elf in the village if she had to, but she liked better to teach martial arts to the elf children so they could defend themselves against wild wolves and other predators they might encounter in the rugged terrain.

The last of the very important leaders in the elf village was Wunorse Openslae who designed Santa's sleigh, and kept it in good running order as well as making sure the reindeer were well taken care of. With his Viking blood, he was a fierce warrior and if needed in any battle he was a great defender against enemy elves of other remote tribes who were banished from society.

Needless to say, Santa had the best team in the world and could not only defend themselves against fierce enemies but could take on almost any task.

The night went on and the north wind blew colder as the campfire sent fireflies of flames into the cold dark. Santa was finishing up the last of thousands of letter that lay at his feet.

"… and the orphanage promised me if I was a good kid this year they would make sure to let Santa know to bring me the greatest gift I could wish for. A guitar to learn to play Christmas songs and write my own beautiful songs I like to sing. Thank you, Santa. Emily."

"Awe, that is so sweet," Sugarplum Mary and hugged her youngest child close to her chest and they had tears in their eyes.

Kids who needed a gift the most on any Christmas were ones without a family. That was a sad thing Santa wish he could fix. Every child should have parents to take care of them.

Santa smiled sadly as he folded the letter and placed it with the large stack of other letter.

"Emily sounds like a sweetheart of a child." Nothing in the world would make Santa' happier than bringing joy to such a special child.

Ardin, a crafty little elf pulled out an old tiny guitar. The guitar was bigger than he, but he seemed determined to play it.

"We can give the orphan girl this guitar, Santa. It was my grandfather's.

"Maybe," Santa smiled and stood up. "I have to get rest now."

"Can I play a song Santa, please?" Continued Ardin.

Santa hesitated but saw the anticipation in his eyes. It was a perfect moment with so many elves gathered by the fire, so how could he deny the joyful request

"Okay, one song."

Santa sat back down.

"Do the little bean boys in the olive tree," a young child elf requested.

His name was Jolla, the son of Bushy Evergreen.

"Okay," said Ardin and he started strumming the guitar.

They all knew the song and like a well-trained choir they all chimed in, including Santa as they sang;

"The little bean boys in the olive tree.

One day fell down on the ground.

Their mommy and daddy were away.

So they knew they were free to play.

But very soon they saw a wolf

And they had to run for their lives

They wished they were back up in the tree

But now they were lost in the weeds... "

** 2 **

<u>DREAMING OF SANTA</u>

The Roberts family all sang together at the

dinner table. It was a new Christmas song from Cole

Son. "All Of Me To You."

"ALL OF ME TO YOU"

Oh, it's been a long, long year.

Waiting for a miracle to appear.

I know you've been wishing for something.

Longing for Christmas to be here."

Dennis and Emma Roberts were having diner

with their daughter and son, Jamie who was ten years

old and Rick who just celebrated his eighth birthday.

The singing stopped and hey clapped hands…

"Very nice," laughed Emma.

They continued eating.

"Pass me the ketchup," Rick asked his sister.

"Please," she responded not looking up from her cellphone as she sent a text.

"Why do I always have to say please?" Rick asked annoyed.

"Because you can't get anything if you don't say please," she answered.

"Stop it, you two." Emma said. "Didn't we just sing a nice Christmas song together? And no texting at the dinner table, Jamie. I told you I'll take the phone for ten days."

"Sorry mom." Jamie stopped texting. "Tell Rick to say please."

"Rick." Emma gave him a stern look.

"No one in school ever says please," he said irritated.

"Well, you're in the wrong school," Dennis replied.

"I hate school," Rick said. "The kids are not good."

Emma gave Dennis a worried look.

Rick took the ketchup Jamie handed him anyway, seeing he was upset.

"Thanks," he said dryly.

"That's good Rick," Emma said looking at her son proudly.

She hesitated as she took her last bite of her food.

"What do you want for Christmas?" Emma asked Rick.

"Nothing," he said and continued eating.

"Nothing?" Dennis asked surprised.

"I want a laptop, dad." Jamie requested.

"Why?" Rick snarled. "So you can sit more on facebook?"

"Don't be stupid," said Jamie.

"I don't want you to waste your time on social media," her father replied. "It's bad for your health and there are bad people on the internet. Hear me, Jamie?"

She nodded.

Denis continued, "you can't trust anyone."

"I want a laptop for designing, dad. Photoshop and pictures." Upset she looked at her mother. "Ma!"

"I'll ask Santa," said Emma.

Rick almost choked in his food laughing.

"Santa is not real!"

"Santa is real!" Yelled Jamie.

"Rick snarled without looking at her, "don't be stupid."

"You're stupid." Jamie threw a plastic spoon at him.

"Stop it you two," Dennis said sternly. "And stop using the word stupid. What did I teach you? That's disrespectful."

"Sorry?" Said Jamie and continued eating.

"Rick, what do you say?" Emma asked her son.

"Sorry," Rick said not looking up from his food.

Emma looked at her children. "There are only a few days left in school. It's almost Christmas and I need you two to be more grateful and respectful, understand?"

No answer.

"Understand?" She commanded more firmly and the kids nodded.

Dennis stood up. "I'm going to bed."

He walked out. Not in the mood for what was happening at the dinner table.

Again, Jamie asked her mother, "can I please get a laptop?"

"I want another school," Rick said upset. "That's what I want."

"Well, Santa don't give away schools, silly," Jamie laughed.

Emma spoke calmly. "Rick, this is the only school near us and we cannot move right now. Your dad isn't making enough money. Do you understand?"

Sympathetically, she took her son's hand.

No answer.

She continued, "besides, next year you'll be in a new class and things will be better."

"It won't." Rick pulled his hand away and darted off to his bedroom.

Emma sighed and looked at Jamie.

"He's upset because he was in a fight," said Jamie.

"I know, and I told him not to fight with the other boys in class. Your father already spoke to his teacher."

She stood up and started with the dishes.

"There are only two days left of school. Next year he'll be in a new class."

In his bedroom, Rick was playing a game on computer. He was a little over his tantrum with his attention was on the game.

"Yeah," he yelled as he fired at the enemy, but suddenly his computer died!

"Damn!" He kicked his desk and saw that the plug had popped out of the computer.

Upset, Rick tumbled onto his bed and he lay there staring up at the ceiling. He knew it was school time in the morning and he was not in the mood for it. He felt emotional and alone, and he started crying.

No one understood how hard it was going to a school you didn't like. Everyday he felt stressed and knew that he might be in a fight with someone he didn't like or someone who didn't like him. He hated school. If only he could be an adult and do what he wants to. He wasn't even in the mood for Christmas if he had to go back to that school next year.

'If he had a wish for Christmas, it would be to have a new school,' he thought.

Rick fell asleep and soon had a dream that he saw Santa with a big smile walking with him to the top of the hill. Behind him were his reindeer attached to the sleigh that had a big bag of toys on top of it. The reindeer were happily eating grass as he and Santa reached the top of the hill.

"This is your Christmas Wish, Rick."

They reached the top of the hill and could now see into the valley below. Before them was a new school in a golden glow of light and the kids were all so happy and joyful, playing in the snow.

"This is your new school where you'll be happy." Santa smiled.

"So you are real then Santa?" Rick asked.

"Oh yes, I am real, Rick. You see, if it weren't for the elves, the reindeer and me, our earth would be a very dark place and there would be no happiness and joy. Who would there be to make children laugh when they were sad, or make them sing with joy, if it weren't for all the Christmas songs that were written about me?"

"I guess, said Rick."

"Rick, can you imagine how unhappy the whole earth would be if there was no wish for good things to come, or a present to be had? Would you want to live on a planet that didn't have those happy moments of Christmas that brought light into the darkness?"

Rick could feel joy well up from inside himself as he gazed at the new school that lay before him. He realized Santa was right. The world would be a very sad place if it weren't for Santa or Christmas.

"So, what is your wish, Rick?"

Rick started to speak but Santa was already back at his sleigh and suddenly the reindeer took off across the sky as they flew away.

"Santa wait!" Rick screamed as tears welled up in his eyes.

Then suddenly, Rick woke up where he lay in his bed. It was quiet and dark and his heart was pounding in his chest. He felt an emptiness inside him he could not explain.

Rick jumped out of his bed and snapped on the light. He sat down on his bed wondering about the strange dream.

"It felt so real," he whispered and his mind was reeling, trying to understand what it all meant.

'The dream felt so real,' he thought as he lay back silently for a long time.

Rick was reliving the joy he felt while he was in the presence of Santa Claus. Just feeling the happiness that he felt made him believe that Santa was real.

***

The next day was very slow at Blowing Rock Elementary School as the atmosphere was one of Christmas and holidays. The kids were dressed in warm clothing in the light snow of North Carolina. Some kids were wearing Christmas type clothing celebrating the Christmas spirit.

The kids couldn't wait for the school day to end and somehow Rick avoided getting into trouble with the bullies in his class. Maybe their parents warned them that if they misbehaved there would be no presents this year.

Rick didn't tell anyone about his dream, but he could not stop thinking of it all day. It was one of the best dreams he had ever had and he wished that Santa was real and that magical things could happen. The world would be a wonderful place then.

Jamie heard the honking of her mother's car and ran towards it looking for Rick. Their parents already picked up most of the kids and some had boarded the various school buses on their way home.

"Rick!" Jamie yelled as she reached the car.

"Where is he?" Emma asked from behind the steering wheel.

"I don't know, mom..."

Just then they saw Rick coming around the corner with one of the bullies in his class and they were laughing and seemed to be in a fun mood.

"What?" Jamie asked out loud. "I don't believe my eyes."

They witnessed Rick doing a fist bump with the bully and then he ran towards them and hopped into the back seat of the car.

"You made friends?" Emma as asked as they were driving home.

"No."

"Well, you were laughing with Barry." Said Jamie. "I thought you hated him?"

Rick hesitated and looked at his cellphone.

"What did he say?" Asked Emma with a light smile on her face.

She felt happy that her kids were okay and that Rick was in a better mood.

"He said Santa was bringing him an Xbox and he said I could come by and play."

"Really?" Asked Emma.

Rick laughed. "And I laughed at him and said Santa was not real."

"Then what?" Asked Emma.

"He didn't even get upset. He just smiled and said, if he continued to be nice till Christmas, his father promised that Santa was bringing him an Xbox."

"See, isn't that great" said Emma.

"Yeah," Rick said dryly and started playing a game on his phone.

"At least something good came out of it, right?" Emma continued.

"Well, then I am sure I am getting a laptop computer seeing I am so nice," Jamie teased and elbowed Rick.

He gave her an annoying bump with his arm to leave him alone.

Jamie was looking at her mom, hopeful that her wish would come true.

** 3 **

THE LAST WISH FULFILLED

Across the world, Christmas carols filled the air as colored lights blazed into the cold night. Christmas evening was in full swing as Santa streaked by like a lightning bolt, dropping off gifts and scurrying in and out of chimneys, delivering good wishes and toys for everyone who asked.

"Tonight we're making a surprise stop, Rudolf," he spoke to his reindeer as the sleigh slipped in behind an orphanage on the far side of a Southern town in Ohio.

Santa leaped from the sleigh with one of his smaller bags, leaving the big bag on the sleigh, and he entered the front door where there was a single glowing Christmas tree. In a large room he saw twelve children with two caretakers singing a Christmas carol. When they saw Santa, the kids yelled happily.

"It's Santa!"

They darted towards the bigger than life figure of Santa and hugged him.

"Hi, children," I'm uncle Joe from next door. "I brought you bags of candy from Sugarplum Mary."

He gave the children all sorts of candy and they also loved the gifts he was handing them.

One boy yelled excitedly. "This is exactly what I wanted! Thanks, Santa."

One of the elderly ladies responded with a heartwarming gesture of gratitude.

"Thanks so nice of you, Uncle Joe..." she caught herself and replied, "Santa."

She really believed it was uncle Joe from next door and didn't want to disappoint the kids.

Santa asked; "and who is Emily?"

A little girl gasped and her hand covered her mouth as she signaled to Santa that it was her.

Santa took a step forward and stroke the hair of the freckled face child. His heart felt warm and emotional as he reached into his bag and pulled out the old special guitar from Ardin.

"This guitar is old, but it is very special," Santa said and Emily took the guitar with tears in her eyes.

"Oh, thank you Santa!" She squealed excitedly as she strummed the guitar.

"This guitar played every song ever written by the fairies and the elves and there is only this one. That's why I am giving it to you. You will write many Christmas songs with this guitar."

Emily kissed Santa on his thick white beard and shared her joy with the other kids.

Santa turned to the two elderly caretakers. "And this is for you my ladies."

He handed them each a small parcel and they knew it was exactly what they asked for this Christmas.

Santa quickly hurried back out to the sleigh as the ladies opened their presents.

One lady held up a heart necklace and was ecstatic.

"How did he know I wanted this?"

"I don't know," replied to other lady as she looked in amazement at exactly the gift she asked for as well. "I can't believe it."

The ladies looked at each other while the children were enjoying their candy and toys.

"Is there an uncle Joe next door?" One of the caretakers asked the other and saw the uncertainty in her eyes.

Then she said, "I think that was the real Santa."

"I write Santa a letter for this guitar, cried Emily."

The two ladies were overwhelmed and shocked. They knew a miracle had occurred and that Santa was real as can be.

Santa smiled as he continued through the night on his sleigh. He liked to play pranks on people, pretending to be just another normal person, like Uncle Joe. No one would ever know then when it was really Santa Claus.

The snow was blowing hard in Alaska when Santa's sleigh streaked into the town of Fairbanks under a blanket of ice. The sleigh touched down behind a barn where the family with three children was anxiously awaiting their toys as they sat teary eyed near the fireplace. They were not sure if they were going to get any toys this year because their daddy had lost his job and their mommy was working very hard at the grocery store to pay the rent and buy food.

They only had a small Christmas tree their father got from their own backyard and there were only three lights on the tree. It was simple but it gave the children a feeling of Christmas, their parents thought. They would do anything to make sure their children were happy.

The kids were playing with a few simple toys when they heard a sound of something slipping down the chimney. Excited, they looked and saw a big box falling on the floor. Luckily there was no fire in the fireplace or the box would have caught on fire.

"What was that?" Their father asked urgently as the children stormed the box and started ripping it open like a pack of wild animals.

"It's Santa." Screamed the older child. "He brought us toys!"

The kids could not believe their eyes when they pulled out smaller boxes addressed to the whole family.

"For daddy," the oldest girl said as she handed the box to her father who was surprised.

"This is mine cried the youngest child as she started ripping open a box addressed to her.

"Ahhhh, it's a Barbie! Just what I wanted! Look at all the dresses!"

"I've got a cellphone!" The oldest girl said excitedly and in amazement saw he mother produce a red dress from her box.

"Just what I wanted," the mother said softly and very surprised. She looked at her husband. "What did you get?"

He did not have the words as he showed her a check for two thousand dollars. The mother's hand went to her mouth. They knew a miracle had occurred and this was a very special Christmas.

What Santa didn't anticipate was the two Terrier Bulldogs that guarded the backyard and when they saw Santa coming out of the chimney and dropping down the side of the house where the reindeer waited patiently with the sleigh, they charged him.

Rudolf the red nosed reindeer was always on the alert for such a thing and he made a loud snarling sound and banged his heavy hoof into the cold ice with a thump. Santa ran as fast as he could and hopped into the sleigh just in time to avoid a bite from the two vicious dogs.

"No presents for you," Santa snapped at the angry dogs. "C'mon, Dasher, Prancer, let's go!"

Santa snapped the reigns and the sleigh jerked forward.

Inside the house, the family heard the commotion outside.

"What was that?" Yelled the middle child Rita as they heard the dogs barking like crazy.

Their father grabbed his shotgun and they darted outside just in time to see the sleigh shooting into the snowstorm.

"It's Santa," screamed the kids!

"It's Santa!" The little girl cried again and waved a goodbye. "Thank you, Santa!"

In amazement and wonder, the father dropped his shotgun and looked at his wife.

"I'll be damned," he said looked down at the happy faces of his children holding their brand new toys.

"This was my Christmas wish," He muttered before they entered back into the house.

Santa covered his face against the blizzard and the reindeer had a hard time finding their direction.

"Good job, guys," Santa encouraged his reindeer and looked at the empty bag in his sleigh. All the toys had been delivered.

Then he remembered something and quickly dug into the inside pocket of his red suit.

"Oh, no," he cried out!

The reindeer looked back at Santa with a "what now", expression on their faces.

"There's one more wish I have to fulfill, boys and girls." He was speaking to the reindeer.

'Christmas is almost over and we're against time!'

The reindeer's thoughts could be heard by Santa. They understood each other very well and they could communicate by mere thought.

Santa said urgently. "We have to hurry back to Blowing Rock, North Carolina?"

"North Carolina!" The Reindeer cried out! "We'll never make it, Santa!"

"It's impossible!" Cried Prancer.

Santa knew this was no going to be easy. "I have never let anyone down and I cannot do it tonight!"

"We were there already, Santa, how will we make it now!" The reindeer expressed their displeasure.

I forgot this wish in my pocket. I am sorry. I must fulfill the wish. He felt a little worried and as the wind and ice blew all around him Santa steered the sleigh and the reindeer back to North Carolina.

Inside the living room of the Roberts family, they had all opened up their gifts and the night was winding down. The clock read eleven forty five pm.

Jamie was on her new laptop while the others were on their phones and watching a choir on the television singing, "We wish you a merry Christmas and a happy new year."

Emma spoke. "Well, Rick you didn't wanted anything for Christmas but we got you that new bicycle anyway you wanted."

"Thanks mom... and dad."

Rick was grateful that he did receive a bicycle but it would take a lot more to make him happy this season. He was still depressed over his school situation and he wished he didn't have to deal with it next year.

"You don't look too happy, said Jamie.

"I am." He said no more.

"You said didn't wanted anything, Rick but at least you got a bicycle."

Emma remembered, "except going to a new school."

"But that is not a gift," said Rick while not looking up from his cellphone.

"No," said Emma. "It's a wish. A wish is the same thing as a gift."

Dennis looked at the clock and stood up.

"Well, Christmas is almost over. Time to go to bed."

Rick shut down his phone and remembered the dream he had about Santa. It was all a lie. This Christmas was not special.

Santa was rushing against time as the sleigh flew as fast as it could towards North Carolina and now he was becoming a little worried."

"We're not going to make it, papa," cried Cupid the reindeer and egged on the others to move faster.

Santa had a trick up his sleeve and he knew he needed magic right now! From underneath the seat of his sleigh, he produced a small bag of magic fairy dust. He knew it was risky as the fairy dust were meant to move only himself through a time portal if he ever needed it and now was the time. But moving himself, the sleigh, reindeer through a time portal could be dangerous.

Santa could now clearly see the face of Samantha, the fairy Goddess who attended his wedding of Santa with the ice-princess. She blessed Santa with this gift.

'You can only use this magical fairy dust one time in a single year. It creates a time portal or tunnel to help you in an emergency situation. The magical fairy dust is connected to time itself, therefore it takes an entire year to become fully potent. Three hundred and sixty five days of the year and every hour, every minute and every second in it.'

'If there ever was an emergency situation this was it,' Santa thought as he tried to remember the magical rhyme to activate the dust.

He though he remembered and said loudly in the cold blast of air.

"Magic, magic of all time. Be at the place where I need to be now."

Three times Santa repeated the spell and then he tossed the dust into the ice cold wind thinking of exactly the address he had to be at. Thanks to the swirling ice wind, the fairy dust circled in a flash all around the sleigh and the reindeer and a magical blue glow engulfed them suddenly.

Wham, the sleigh touched down right on the roof of the Roberts family.

It was now three minutes before midnight and Santa had to rush down the chimney and he snuck the letter he had in his pocket into the shirt of Dennis. In his Rush, Santa tripped over a stool and fell to the floor with a bang.

'Oh, No!' He quickly got up.

"What was that?" He heard Emma's voice as she came out of the bedroom.

Santa hurried quickly up the chimney and Emma though she saw a piece of red coat disappearing into the chimney.

Surprised, she rushed over and looked into the chimney but there was nothing.

"What is it?" She heard Dennis' voice and she noticed his work shirt lying on the floor and the letter sticking out of it.

Emma picked up the letter and saw that it was addressed to Dennis.

"Dennis, you have a letter in our shirt."

She walked into the bedroom and handed it to her husband where she lay in bed.

"Oh, I forgot about it," he said and opened it.

It was from his employer and he read out aloud,

"Congratulations on your achievements this year, Dennis. The company decided to award you a bonus as well as a transfer to Washington, DC.

"What?" Dennis' jaw dropped to the floor.

This was a huge surprise as this is exactly where Denis and Emma really wanted to live.

"Washington!" Said Emma. "That's where we always wanted to live.

"I know," said Dennis and immediately Emma rushed into Rick's bedroom.

"Ricky!"

"What mom?" He was half asleep and running his eyes as he looked at hr.

"Guess what?"

"What"

You're going to a new school in Washington next year.

"No way?"

"Yes, way. We're moving to Washington."

Excited, Rick hugged his mother."

Thanks, mom!"

They heard the clock chime and looked.

Christmas was over!

Santa and the Reindeer felt proud of what they had accomplished.

"How did you do it, Santa?" Asked Rudolf as they trotted against the black sky.

"Magic, Rudolf. Pure Magic."

Santa felt tired but he smiled satisfied as they careened across the dark skies towards the North Pole.

***

No one worked harder than Santa over this Christmas season, to prepare all the toys and make sure he never made a mistake. To delivered exactly the right toy to the right kid who had wished for it. Oh, my word. It was an unimaginable feat. A task so large that only Santa could do this and no other man, and because of this and age creeping up fast now on Santa, he felt maybe he needed someone to take over the reigns. He felt tired, but what would this do to the world. That was a big concern.

Every year Santa felt it more. He didn't think the entire world's population could understand the toll a task this large could take on someone. His time was coming to an end and he needed someone to take over. He needed a kid who was super strong; super powerful and super fast, and he had just the kid in mind. Who could it be?

His very own, of course! Yes, he finally had a son that was getting just old enough where by next Christmas he would probably be ready to take over this enormous job and be worthy of it. Or maybe he could just ride along in the beginning and help drop some toys. Santa hadn't totally made up his mind yet but it was a promising though.

Kris was his name. A tall, handsome and athletic seventeen year old. He had his mother's eyes. The ice princess and goddess of the fairies. Yes, she was Santa's secret wife and lover all these years and no human knew of it. The elves knew but they were sworn to secrecy and not let the human world know anything of the handsome boy, fathered by Santa with his beloved ice princess.

When Santa lost he first Mrs. Claus, it was a sad moment for the whole elf village and it took years before Santa finally met the ice princess of the very far north and she became his wife.

Every year around Christmas, the ice princess made sure that that there was enough snow and ice around the world so that the reindeer would not perish from their tiring journey around the globe delivering the toys. Imagine if it were too hot, they would not make it, so the ice-princess' role was very important in the North Pole.

"Ho, Ho, ho," Santa egged on his reindeer as he noticed a streak of sunlight starting to appear on the horizon.

The reindeer flew as fast as they could, for they knew, it was almost time to rest for a while. Their hard worked was done for this Christmas. But, the reindeer knew they would fly again soon.

It was time to go home.

***

It was nighttime in the North Pole and Santa was finishing up telling stories to elves around the fire. They were curious to how everything went and if the children appreciated all the hard work the elves had done thought the year to make the toys for them.

"Are you coming to eat my love," Santa heard a voice from his house. "It's getting very late and you must be tired?"

Santa looked at the beautiful ice princess who stood there in the yellowing light of their front porch and the icy breeze played with her long silky blonde hair. She had on a light icy blue gown all the way to her bare feet and she looked like an angel sent from heaven.

"Yes, my love, I'm on my way." Santa said and started rising.

"Thank you, all the elves and the fairies who helped make this a magical Christmas.

"Yeah!" The elves cried overjoyed and clapped their hands together as Santa walked slowly towards his home. He felt very tired.

Santa got out of the well deserved hot tub that was prepared for him by his wife. The inside of Santa's house felt cozy and warm considering the ice-cold weather outside. It had thick hand painted carpets, rows and rows of book-shelves with many ancient books and old fairytales and there were every old paintings decorating the thick wooden log walls.

Santa got into bed beside his wife as she smiled at him.

"It must have been an amazing Christmas?"

"Yes it was." Santa smiled at her and picked up one of his favorite books from the shelf beside his bed. Hansel and Gretel.

Santa started reading when they heard a voice.

"Goodnight poppa. Goodnight mom."

They saw their handsome son standing in the doorway almost bigger than the frame. He was already in his favorite apple tree pajamas and elf like slippers with upward pointed toes.

"Goodnight son," Santa said.

"You're not going out to the elf dance party tonight, son?" Asked the ice princess.

"Not tonight. I'm bored with it."

They knew he was longing for company of his own size as he was much larger than the elves. He wanted to meet humans of his size.

"I know, son." Said Santa. "Soon there'll be exciting things for you to do."

"Like what? Making more toys?" He smiled. When can I take out the sleigh by myself so I can visit other humans?"

Santa thought for a moment not taking his eyes off the book.

"I have something in mind son."

"Like what?" Asked Kris.

I will let you know soon in the next year."

"Well, it's Christmas. Don't I get a Christmas wish?" He asked light heartedly.

"You have everything you need son," said the ice princess as she cuddled into her pillow, ready to go to sleep.

"Except company of my own size, momma."

"I know, my son." She smiled at him.

"Let's just say, you have a big surprise coming next year, son," said Santa with a smile.

With that said, they all went to sleep.

Santa lay awake for a long time thinking. He had a big decision to make for next year and he need to know if it would be the right idea for the world.

Santa knew it would be a big change for the world to realize his son would be the next Santa, because so many generations were used to the idea that Santa was a grown man and a father figure to so many children. He knew his son would have big shoes to fill and he was sure, he would be ready or even if children would still be excited to see him. But because of his good upbringing, and having looked after his mother and all the elves every time Santa went on his Christmas journeys, Kris was mature and related to children very well.

Not only was Kris sensitive to the wishes of children and had the knowledge to fulfill their dreams, but also he was strong enough that he could very well be a father figure to any child who needed it.

Santa thought of the very special red suit that was being prepared for years by the elves just for Kris. It had to be a special suit, just like that of Santa, so that it could withstand all types of weather conditions and all types of adventures Santa could encounter along his treacherous journey every year around the world.

Could you imagine, the weather storms, volcanoes, tornados, smog and pollution around the world and eve fires and many other potential hazards that could stop Santa from fulfilling his task? Yes, the suits had to be strong, durable, adaptable and most importantly protective against anything that might harm Santa. But the new Santa outfit would e far, far more advanced and would have amazing capabilities to enhance the functions of Santa.

And then there was the perfect white beard, yes, Kris would have to wear the beard just like daddy or else children would never recognize him. There were too many people wearing red clothing around Christmas and even though there were Santa impersonators, No one had the perfect beard just like Santa.

Yes, Kris would be the perfect suited Santa to take over next year if that was so to be. It was surely going to be interesting.

Santa fells asleep.

THE END

(Song written by Cole Son)

The Santa Toy Story

Had never been told

In all its glory

The truth behold

The magic of Christmas

Awakens again

The elves in the village

Want you to know

How hard they're working

Throughout the year

To make every wish come true

For everyone

#ColeSon

#ColeSonBooks

Youtube: #ColeSonMusic

www.amazon.com/author/coleson

www.TheSantaToyStory.com

Image Credits:

Jaymzart (pixabay)

Jggraphicstj (pixabay)

Cover Design: Cole Son

www.TheSantaTOYStory.com

www.amazon.com/author/coleson

www.twitter.com/colesonbooks

www.instagram.com/colesonbooks

www.facebook.com/colesonmusic

Made in the USA
Middletown, DE
29 January 2021